Beyond Smiles

Discovering True Happiness

Copyright © 2025 Michelle Mushtaq

All rights reserved

No part of this book may be reproduced, or stored in a retrieval system, or transmitted in any form or by any means, electronic, mechanical, photocopying, recording, or otherwise, without express written permission of the publisher.

ISBN- 978-0-646-73017-2

Cover Copyright: www.thehealingjourney.com.au

Self-Published

website: www.thehealingjourney.com.au

Table Of Contents

1. ## Happiness Is Independent   22
   - ❖ The Spark of Hope
   - ❖ The Cracks Beneath the Surface
   - ❖ The Mirror Moment
   - ❖ Unlearning the old story
   - ❖ Redefining Love and Happiness
   - ❖ What I Know Now

2. ## Love, Lost & Found   39
   - ❖ My Foundation
   - ❖ Lost
   - ❖ When The Foundation Cracks
   - ❖ The Spiral
   - ❖ The Illusion of Relief

- ❖ The Encounter
- ❖ Found
- ❖ Peace and Acceptance
- ❖ Blessing In Disguise

3. Borrowed Happiness   66

- ❖ Giving to borrow happiness
- ❖ Learning to pour back into myself
- ❖ True happiness is not transactional

4. The Illusion Of Happiness   77

- ❖ The smiling mask
- ❖ The Illusion
- ❖ Behind the smile
- ❖ The pressure to be happy
- ❖ Learning to be real
- ❖ The truth beneath the illusion

5. When Purpose Found Me   103
- ❖ The whisper of meaning
- ❖ From giving to growing
- ❖ The calling becomes clear
- ❖ The decision that changed everything
- ❖ Becoming the purpose
- ❖ The peace of alignment

6. The If & When Trap   126
- ❖ The mirage of tomorrow
- ❖ The only time that exist
- ❖ Learning to live in the now

7. Beyond Comparison   138
- ❖ A shout-out to my roots
- ❖ The thief of joy
- ❖ The balance within

8. Searching Happiness, Finding Contentment   147

- ❖ The difference we often miss
- ❖ The lantern and the flame
- ❖ What I know now

9. The PERMA Of My Journey — 158
- ❖ When life becomes the classroom

10. Beyond Smiles — 164
- ❖ The truth behind the smile
- ❖ What I learnt about happiness
- ❖ The essence of "Beyond Smiles"
- ❖ A message to you

Epilogue

Acknowledgement Of Inspiration

About The Author

"Mama and Baba, This one's for you. Without you I wouldn't have been, Without your support nothing that I do would have been."

Author's Note

This book was never meant to be perfect — because my healing wasn't.

When I lived these moments, they didn't unfold in a straight line.
There was no clear beginning, middle, or end.
One season blurred into another — learning, forgetting, pausing, rising, falling, and trying again. Nothing about my journey was neat or chronological. And so, this book reflects the truth of how it happened.

The chapters aren't arranged in order because my life didn't happen in order. I didn't move from confusion to clarity in a clean progression. I didn't learn a lesson once and closed it forever. Some understandings arrived early, some arrived much later, and some drifted in and out until they finally made sense.

Healing didn't come in steps for me —
it came in loops.

If this book feels non-linear, it's because this is the most honest way to tell it. I wrote each chapter in the same order it became real to me — not reorganised for coherence, not softened to look pretty, and not rearranged to create a polished arc. I kept it as I lived them..

Certain parts of my life include Depression and Generalised Anxiety Disorder,
but this is not a book centred on those experiences. They appear only because they existed in the background of my story — not because they define the story. What shaped these pages far more deeply were the moments of shift: the quiet realisations, the internal turning points, the small awakenings,

the lessons that arrived uninvited and changed me anyway.

This book is not about suffering —
It's about what came after.
About rediscovering myself, understanding happiness differently,
and learning how life reshapes us in ways we don't notice until much later.

I didn't write this book as a counsellor.
I wrote it as a human being who was trying to understand her own heart. Someone who was piecing together meaning, learning to breathe through difficult seasons, and slowly discovering a version of herself she didn't know existed yet.

This book holds the most honest and vulnerable version of me.

If you find yourself revisiting certain emotions in these pages — reflection, uncertainty, renewal, hope

— it's because those were the emotions I returned to as well. Some lessons echo through our lives. Some truths grow slowly. Some understandings ask for time.

My hope is not that this book gives you answers.
My hope is that it gives you space —
space to breathe,
space to pause,
space to be gentle with yourself,
space to recognise the shifts happening within you too.

As you read, I don't just want you to follow my story;
I hope you quietly notice your own.
The moments where a sentence touches a memory,
where a realisation mirrors something you've felt,
where a question sounds like the ones you've kept inside.

What are you learning about yourself lately?
What are you holding behind your own smile?

Your story matters just as much — every small change, every quiet courage, every moment of becoming that no one else sees.
This book isn't about having it all figured out.
It's about discovering meaning while still in the middle of it all.
It's about finding a softer, truer version of happiness — one that grows from understanding, not perfection.

This isn't a guide.
It's a witness.
A testament to shifting, growing, and emerging — even when the process is messy or interrupted.

Thank you for being here.
Thank you for opening these pages with an open heart.
Thank you for trusting me with your time and your presence.
Picking up a book about happiness when you may

not feel very close to it is a quiet act of hope —
and sometimes, hope is where everything begins.

— **Michelle**

Preface

It's October 2022. I had just come home from work, exhausted and emotionally drained, shoes still on, my bag thrown carelessly on the couch as I pressed my phone against my ear while speaking with my mother. The conversation had started innocently enough—catching up on the day, discussing mundane family matters—but then it took a turn I wasn't prepared for.

"Michnu," she said, her voice carrying that particular tone of concern that only a mother can have, "you used to drink on weekends or socially, maybe at a party or dinner with friends, but now you've started drinking every day. This isn't healthy. This isn't you.

Promise me you're not going to drink every day anymore."

And I did promise her. Without hesitation, I made her that promise while simultaneously walking toward the refrigerator, my hand already reaching for the handle, grabbing another bottle of beer, twisting off the cap with practiced ease, gulping down the cold alcohol as it burned its way down my throat, all while assuring her with false confidence in my voice that I wouldn't be drinking as much going forward. The words came out smoothly, convincingly even, as if I actually believed them myself.

That was my lowest point—not because I was drinking, not even because of the quantity or frequency, but because I was lying straight to the face of the person who trusted me the most in this world. The person who had raised me, sacrificed for me, believed in me unconditionally. I wasn't just lying to my mother. I was making a promise I knew deep down I couldn't keep, wouldn't keep. Even as the words left my mouth, I knew they were hollow.

The call ended with her usual "I love you" and "take care of yourself," and I stood there in my dimly lit apartment with a half-empty bottle of beer in my hand, feeling the weight of my deception settling heavily on my shoulders. I hadn't even taken off my shoes or changed out of my work clothes before I started drinking. That had become my new routine—walk through the door, head straight for the fridge, crack open a bottle before doing anything else. I finished the bottle mechanically, changed my clothes, freshened up in a daze, and went to bed with more bottles beside me on the nightstand.

I remember sitting there on the edge of my bed, staring at the wall in the semi-darkness, thinking, *What's happening to me? Who have I become?*

I was never this person. Growing up, I was the responsible one, the dependable one. I would move mountains for my parents without a second thought, do anything to make them proud, yet here I was—breaking their trust, shattering my own promises, drowning myself slowly in a bottle, night after night after night.

I was using alcohol to escape. Escape from what exactly, I didn't know at the time—but it felt like everything. I just wanted to come home, get drunk as quickly as possible, and hit the sack—numb, detached, quiet, unreachable. The alcohol provided a temporary refuge, a brief respite from whatever it was I was running from.

On paper, my life was fine. Better than fine, actually. I had a stable job with decent pay, good health with no serious medical issues, a supportive and loving family who checked in on me regularly, and enough financial security to live comfortably without constant worry about bills or expenses. By most objective measures, I was doing well. I had what many people dream of having.

But I wasn't happy. Far from it. Why? What was I trying so desperately to escape from? It took time and painful self-reflection to understand that it was the emptiness inside, the gnawing void that couldn't be filled by external success, material comfort, or numbing substances. I had achieved the markers of success that society tells us matter, but they meant nothing when I looked in the mirror. I needed to find something deeper, something more meaningful: true happiness, genuine fulfillment, a sense of purpose that went beyond just going through the motions each day.

And then the journey began...

1

Happiness is Independent

"No one else can complete you; they can only complement the happiness you already hold."

Marriage... it sounds like the perfect solution, doesn't it?

The idea that finding a life partner could fill the emptiness, could bring that elusive happiness we've all been searching for. I used to turn that thought over and over in my mind: *Maybe getting married will be the answer. Maybe finding the right person will finally make me happy.*

I imagined it vividly — building a life together, sharing mornings and mid-nights, laughing at the same old jokes, facing challenges hand in hand. It seemed so peaceful, so right. Movies, family, social media, even casual conversations echoed the same message: *find your other half, and happiness will follow.*

Everyone seemed to agree that marriage was the ultimate goal, the final piece of the puzzle that would make life complete. The narrative was everywhere, impossible to escape, woven into the fabric of everything I consumed and every conversation I had.

And for a while, I believed it.

The Spark of Hope

I started talking to someone who was also looking for marriage. On paper, everything aligned. We shared values, goals, and a similar vision of what partnership should look like. Conversations flowed easily; his presence felt familiar and safe. I caught myself smiling while texting, waiting eagerly for the next call. It felt like warmth after a long winter, and for the first time in a while, I thought, *maybe this is what happiness feels like. Maybe this is the beginning of something.*

It all made sense.
It *should* have made me happy.

But slowly, unexpectedly, something inside me began to shift.

There was a quiet uneasiness growing beneath the surface — a discomfort I couldn't name.

The closer things got to becoming real, the more this unsettling feeling rose within me.

And then, without warning, the tears began.

I cried during our calls, I cried afterward — curled up in bed, confused and overwhelmed.
I cried while speaking to my parents, who listened to me between their own confusion and concern.

They would ask in the softest voices,

"Why are you crying, Mich? Everything is going exactly as you wanted."

And I had no answer.

How do you explain a feeling you don't understand yourself?

How do you articulate a fear you haven't fully met yet?

On the outside, everything was perfect.

But inside, something was deeply unsettled.

The Cracks Beneath the Surface

It took time and a lot of uncomfortable silence to understand those tears. For a while, I kept trying to find a logical explanation, something that made sense. But every time I tried to blame the situation or the pace or the conversations, the truth kept circling back to the same place:

The tears weren't about him.

They weren't even about "us."

They were about me.

Each tear carried the weight of a truth I wasn't ready to face. A truth I had been tiptoeing around for years:

the space inside me was still hollow — untouched, unhealed — no matter how kind or compatible someone else might be.

I didn't realise it at the time, but I was expecting another person to walk in and magically fill a void that wasn't theirs to fix. I was asking someone, unknowingly, to soothe wounds they didn't cause, to carry emotions they didn't understand, to be an anchor for storms they had never witnessed.

And that's the thing —
he didn't even know that burden existed.
How could he?
I didn't even fully understand it myself.

When that connection eventually ended, I genuinely thought it would break me. I had grown used to his presence — the daily conversations, the predictable warmth of good morning messages, the ease of having someone to share the small pieces of my day with. I assumed losing that comfort would hurt deeply, but strangely… it didn't.

There was sadness, yes.
A quiet ache where the routine used to be.
But no devastation.
No collapse.
No spiraling grief that swallowed me whole.

And in that calm — that surprising stillness after what I thought would be heartbreak — something inside me shifted.

The peace startled me.

Because it revealed something I had missed all along:
what I felt with him wasn't depth — it was distraction.

It wasn't love.
It wasn't alignment.
It was comfort.
It was the feeling of being chosen, seen, and valued — feelings I had been searching for within myself but hadn't fully found yet.

The warmth we shared wasn't rooted. It was soft, fleeting, momentary — a reflection of my longing, not of my wholeness.

And maybe that was the lesson.

I realised I wasn't in love with him...
I was in love with the version of myself I felt when someone else made me feel significant.
I was in love with being seen — not with the person seeing me.

That truth hit harder than the ending itself.

The Mirror Moment

After the relationship ended, I remember one quiet evening sitting with my journal, staring at a blank page. For the first time, I wrote without filters, without worrying how it would sound if someone else read it:
Why do I believe love will save me? Why am I afraid of being alone?

The answers came slowly, painfully honest. I wasn't afraid of loneliness — I was afraid of meeting myself there.

If that relationship had continued, I might have kept searching for happiness through someone else's presence...
placing my wholeness in their hands...
depending on their affection to feel enough.

And that would have been unfair —
to him, and more importantly, to me.

Looking back now, I see it clearly:

That ending was divine timing.

God's gentle way of saying,

"You can't love him yet — because you are still learning how to love yourself."

That ending wasn't a wound; it was wisdom.

I realised that what I was truly seeking wasn't a person; it was peace. A sense of wholeness that didn't depend on someone else's presence or approval. I didn't want marriage; I wanted meaning. And no one; not the kindest heart, not the closest connection — could hand that to me.

That awareness didn't arrive as an epiphany; it unfolded gently over time. Through moments of discomfort, through learning to enjoy my own company, through evenings that felt both empty and freeing.

I started doing small things for myself — morning walks without my phone, journaling with honesty instead of perfection, saying "no" when I used to say "yes" just to be liked or to avoid disappointing someone. At first, it all felt awkward — like trying to build a relationship with a stranger I had lived with my entire life.
It felt vulnerable, tender, unfamiliar.

But slowly I noticed — it began to rebuild me.

Unlearning the Old Story

For most of my life, I'd absorbed the idea that happiness is shared, that we're halves searching for completion, incomplete puzzle pieces drifting through the world looking for our perfect match.

Phrases like "You make me happy" or "I can't be happy without you" sounded so innocent, even romantic. They were woven into every love song, every movie, every story I'd ever consumed about what love was supposed to look like.

I used to say them too — not realising how heavy they actually were. Because what we don't realise is that every time we say "you make me happy," we quietly hand over the power to someone else. We put the weight of our emotional wellbeing on their shoulders and ask them to carry something that was never theirs to carry. We make them responsible for our internal weather, for our sense of wholeness, for filling the empty spaces we haven't learned to fill ourselves.

And maybe that's why so many of us break under the pressure of love—because we expect others to hold what only we can build. We turn people into our anchors and call it connection, when really, it's just dependency dressed as affection. We mistake the temporary relief of distraction for genuine fulfillment. We confuse the dopamine rush of new attention with lasting contentment. And when they inevitably fail to sustain our happiness—because no human being ever could—we feel betrayed, abandoned, lost. We blame them for not being enough, when the truth is we were asking the impossible.

It took me years—and a few heartbreaks—to understand that happiness isn't borrowed. It's built. Real happiness isn't found in someone's words, attention, or presence, no matter how consistent or loving they are. It's found in the quiet steadiness within you, the part that stays even when everything else leaves. It's the foundation you build through self-awareness, through healing, through learning to sit with yourself without needing someone else to make the silence bearable. It's cultivated in small moments of self-compassion, in boundaries you honor, in promises you keep to yourself when no one's watching.

Love, when it's healthy, doesn't make you happy. It meets you in your happiness. It grows beside it. It celebrates it, nurtures it, respects it. But it doesn't carry it. It doesn't create it from nothing. Healthy love is two whole people choosing to walk together, not two broken

halves desperately clinging to each other for survival.
That was the story I had to unlearn — that happiness isn't something someone gives you. It's something you discover when you finally stop asking others to complete you. When you stop searching outside yourself for what can only be found within. When you realize that the love you've been seeking in others is the same love you've been withholding from yourself.

Redefining Love and Happiness

With time, I began to see love differently. Love isn't about completion; it's about companionship between two already-whole people. It's not about finding someone who makes the world brighter, but about walking alongside someone while you both keep your own light alive.

When we learn to be content within ourselves, relationships stop being cages of expectation. They become spaces of freedom and sharing. There's no pressure to perform, no anxiety about losing yourself, no constant fear of abandonment. Instead, there's breathing room. There's trust. There's the quiet confidence that comes from knowing you'll be okay, no matter what.

You no longer need someone to make you happy; you *choose* to share your happiness with them. That shift changes everything.It transforms relationships from survival mechanisms into genuine connections.

Happiness, I learned, is independent. It isn't fragile or fleeting when it's built from the inside out. I started listening to my own voice, trusting my own instincts, honoring my own needs and boundaries.
It's rooted in self-awareness, nurtured by self-acceptance, and sustained by truth. The deeper I went into understanding myself, the less dependent I became on external validation.

Now, when I think about marriage, it no longer feels like the missing piece to my puzzle. It feels like something that could be beautiful — but not necessary for my wholeness. I'm already complete. I'm already enough. Marriage, if it comes, would be a choice made from abundance, not scarcity. From desire, not desperation. If it happens, it will be an addition, not an answer. And that distinction makes all the difference.

What I Know Now

Looking back, I can see that the tears weren't weakness; they were wisdom trying to reach me. They were the voice of my inner self saying, *"You're not ready to give what you haven't found yet."* Those tears weren't born from sadness alone — they came from a deeper place, a part of me that understood something my conscious mind couldn't yet accept. They were a signal, a gentle warning that I was trying to build my life on someone else's foundation instead of my own. And that voice was right. Happiness that depends on another person will always be fragile. It's like building a house on sand — beautiful in the moment, but doomed to crumble when the tides of life shift. When your joy is tethered to someone else's presence, their moods, their choices, their love — you become a passenger in your own life, endlessly waiting for permission to feel whole. But happiness that's built within you — that's unshakable. It weathers storms. It survives disappointments. It remains steady even when everything around you changes.Today, my happiness doesn't hinge on who stays, who leaves, or who understands. It's rooted in knowing who I am when the world is silent. It's in small things — making coffee in peace, watching sunsets alone without feeling lonely, knowing I'm enough without needing anyone to prove it. It's in the quiet mornings when I wake up and feel grateful just to be alive. It's in the realization that solitude isn't emptiness — it's space to grow, to breathe, to become.

So, if there's one thing I've learned, it's this:

No one else can complete you — because you were never incomplete. You were always whole, even when you felt broken. You were always enough, even when the world told you otherwise. Love may walk beside you, but happiness must live within you. Love is a companion, not a savior. It can enrich your life, add color to your days, bring warmth to your nights — but it cannot and should not be the source of your peace. That's a job only you can do.

2

Love, Lost and Found!

"Sometimes the hardest goodbyes are the ones that don't get said — the ones that echo in silence."

Love doesn't always leave quietly.

Sometimes it rips through your life like a storm — not the romantic kind, but the kind of love that feels like home, sacred, steady, irreplaceable. And when that kind of love leaves, it does not just hurt you – it HURTS YOU! to the point you physically feel the pain in every inch of your body, from the tips of your fingers to the depths of your chest. It's a pain that radiates outward, consuming everything in its path, making it hard to breathe, hard to think, hard to simply exist

The words *"my heart is broken"* stop being a metaphor — they become terrifyingly real. that you actually feel your heart being shattered into pieces inside of you, like pieces of glass – sharp and edgy and each sharp point of the piece rips everything in your body making you feel every bit of the pain in excruciating detail. You become intimately acquainted with suffering in a way you never thought possible, in a way that changes you forever.

LOVE

I have always been someone who is very family oriented. My world revolves around the family, the people who raised me, shaped me, and stood by me through every high and low. I never thought I could love someone as much as I love my family, or that anyone could affect me as deeply, as profoundly, as much as my parents and siblings do.

But then, about a year after I was diagnosed with **Generalized Anxiety Disorder (GAD) and Depression**, when my internal world felt fragile and confusing, this person entered my life. Let's just call her Ahaana.

Her presence came with a quiet strength that didn't demand attention but commanded respect. Her calm, non-judgmental personality was the solace I desperately needed during a time of such emotional upheaval. The way she used to meet me where I was; whether I was cracking jokes or crying in frustration, whether I needed intellectual stimulation or just someone to sit with me in silence— she became my anchor.

From banter to teaching me, guiding me, mentoring me to laughing with me, to wiping my tears when the world felt too heavy—she became HOME! She became FAMILY. She truly became my mother figure. **My Ahaana Mama**.

I often told her that I saw so much of my father in her; the same gentle firmness, the same unwavering principles, the same ability to discipline with love. Maybe that's why she fit so perfectly into that role without ever trying to, without ever forcing it. It was organic, natural, like she was always meant to be there, bridging the gap left by my struggle.

I love my real mom to death, unconditionally and fiercely but my mom and I have always shared more of a friendship relationship, where she was my best friend, my confidante, the person I'd gossip with and share secrets with. Amongst my parents, my father was the one who played the role of the authoritative parental figure; the one that would scold us when needed to discipline us and school us while still being the gentle and loving parent. Which is exactly what I saw in Ahaana Mama too, schooling me and scolding me when I needed it most, even when I didn't want to hear it. She had that right, and I gladly gave it to her. Because I trusted her completely, implicitly, with my whole heart. And she knew she could do that and that was what was good for me at the moment and what would not be right.

It was just beautiful, having someone to guide me through life's complexities, to tell me right from wrong without sugar-coating things, to call me out when needed without making me feel small, to be a shoulder to lean on during my darkest hours and also being someone I could totally be my childish, silly, unfiltered self with. Someone who saw all of me—the good, the bad, the embarrassing—and was there for me anyway, particularly during a period when I felt inherently flawed.

Addressing her as **"mama"** just became my solace, my safe space, my anchor. And she would often call me **"Bache"** *(Translates to: baby, kid, child)*. Every single time she said it, it carried warmth. Care. Acceptance. It made me feel seen, truly seen for who I was beneath all the masks and defenses, as if she was reminding me, *"You're safe here. You don't have to be strong all the time. You can just be you."*

MY FOUNDATION

She was, in every sense, a mother figure — the kind of

person whose presence made the world quieter, softer, more bearable. Around her, I felt safe enough to be unguarded, to let down the walls I'd spent years building. She had this way of making everything feel less urgent, less heavy. Just being near her was calming, like stepping into a warm room after being out in the cold for too long.

She was also one of the very few people — apart from my father — who I truly *listened to*. Not just heard, but *listened*. She could scold me, and I wouldn't get defensive. I wouldn't argue back or shut down the way I did with most people. Her words carried weight because they came from care, not judgment. She never spoke to tear me down; she spoke to build me up, even when that meant pointing out where I'd gone wrong.

I've always been strong-willed, stubborn even, the one who leads and makes decisions without needing approval or input from others. But with her, I didn't need to lead. I didn't need to be in control or have all the answers. I could just *be*. And that kind of surrender didn't make me weak; it made me feel protected.

That's why I told her, *"You're my foundation."*
Because she was. The person who made me believe that people outside of family could be family too. That chosen family is just as real, just as vital, as blood. But nothing lasts forever. And that truth, as much as I tried to ignore it, was always waiting.

LOST

In 2022, I lost her. I lost someone who wasn't family by blood, but she was my foundation. She wasn't just a part of my life; she was the grounding presence I leaned on when everything else felt uncertain. I trusted her deeply — maybe more than I ever trusted anyone before.
I remember telling her once, *"I'm scared to love deeply because people always leave."*
It wasn't something I said lightly. It came from years of watching people drift away, of learning that sometimes promises don't last.

She smiled and said, *"I'm not going anywhere."* And I believed her. With everything in me, I did.

For the first time in a long time, love didn't feel like a risk. It felt like home.

When the Foundation Cracks

There was no confrontation, no clear ending — just silence that stretched until it became permanent. No dramatic fight, no final phone call, no closure of any kind. Just the slow, agonizing realization that the person I'd trusted most had simply... disappeared. Days turned into weeks, and the silence grew heavier, more suffocating, until I finally understood: they weren't coming back.

It felt like something inside me had shattered into a thousand pieces. I cried for weeks — the kind of crying that aches in your chest, that leaves you hollow and exhausted. The kind that sneaks up on you in the middle of mundane tasks: washing dishes, driving to work, lying awake at 3 AM staring at the ceiling. I replayed conversations over and over in my mind, analyzing every word, every pause, every facial expression I could remember. I wondered what I had done wrong, what I could've said differently, whether there was some invisible line I'd crossed without realizing it.But there were no answers. Only emptiness. Only the deafening quiet where a relationship used to be. Only questions that would never be answered and apologies that would never be heard.And somewhere in that pain, buried beneath the confusion and hurt, I realized I had done what I always feared: I'd placed my happiness in someone else's hands. I'd made them responsible for my sense of worth, my feeling of belonging. And when they left, they took all of that with them.

The Spiral

Days blurred together in a hazy fog of routine and sadness. I tried to talk about it with my friends, seeking some kind of validation or understanding, but every time I did, someone would inevitably say, *"Michelle, she wasn't your partner,"* as if that made the grief less real, less legitimate, less worthy of acknowledgment. They didn't understand that love doesn't need a title to leave a wound. It doesn't need labels or official recognition to carve out a space in your heart that aches when it's gone.

So I stopped talking about it. I stopped reaching out. I turned inward, and sometimes, downward. The silence became suffocating, and I filled it with anything that numbed it — habits that felt compulsive, distractions that offered temporary relief, and even something I never thought I would do in a million years — psychic readings. I found myself desperately searching for answers, for closure, for any sign that what I felt mattered.

The Illusion of Relief

After she left, the silence was unbearable. It wasn't just the absence of her messages or calls — it was the absence of her voice, her warmth, her grounding presence that had become part of my every day.

And because I couldn't talk to anyone about it — not really — I started finding other ways to fill that void. My friends wouldn't understand the complexity of what we had. My family would be hurt seeing me hurt. So I kept it all locked inside, where it festered and grew heavier with each passing day. Little distractions, small comforts, anything that could make me feel less alone for a few minutes.

That's when I found myself reaching for temporary relief. Some nights it was a drink — just one at first, then two, then however many it took to dull the edges of the pain. Other nights it was booking a psychic reading — chasing the next comforting line, the next "She'll come back," the next moment of false certainty that maybe, just maybe, this wasn't really over. I'd spend money I didn't have, staying up until 3 AM talking to strangers on the internet who claimed they could see my future, who promised reconnection and reconciliation.

It wasn't about believing everything I was told. I'm not naive — I knew most of it was generic, scripted, designed to keep me coming back. It was about how those words made me feel for a few moments — seen, reassured, less hollow. Someone was telling me what I desperately wanted to hear, and in those brief exchanges, the crushing weight of her absence lifted just enough for me to breathe. I was trapped in the vicious cycle of **"Instant gratification"**

But the thing about instant comfort is that it fades as quickly as it comes. The high would wear off, reality would come crashing back, and I'd be left feeling even more empty than before — plus guilty, ashamed, and increasingly desperate for the next fix.

When the readings ended, the quiet came back — heavier than before.

And so I'd do it again.

Just one more reading, one more scroll, one more message to the universe asking for a sign. And let me tell you—I spent hundreds, no, *thousands* of dollars on something I deep down always believed was pseudo.

It took me a while to understand that this was my way of avoiding the pain — of trying to fix an ache that needed to be felt, not covered.

I was searching for her in other people's voices, hoping they'd say the one thing she never did: that it wasn't really over.

But deep down, I knew the truth.

What I was missing wasn't her presence anymore — it was the peace that used to come from it. And no one else could give me that.

That was the beginning of a hard, slow lesson — that real healing doesn't come from escape. It comes from sitting with the emptiness until it starts to lose its power.

The Encounter

One afternoon, feeling suffocated by the weight of my own thoughts and desperately needing air, I went to a small coffee shop. I just wanted a place that I hadn't been before to just feel new and different.

A woman sat near me at the next table, close enough

that when she made a casual comment about the weather, it didn't feel intrusive. That small exchange turned into conversation. We talked about nothing in particular at first – the kind of surface-level chat strangers have when they're both seeking connection without really knowing why. Over time, over the course of several weeks, we kept bumping into each other at that same coffee shop, talking a little more each time. It became our unspoken routine, a strange comfort in the midst of my chaos.

One day, after we'd known each other for about a month, she looked at me – really looked at me – with eyes that seemed to see past all the walls I'd carefully constructed, and asked, *"Have you recently lost someone you dearly love?"*

Her words stopped me cold. My breath caught in my throat, and for a moment I couldn't speak. *"How can you tell?"* I finally asked, my voice barely above a whisper.

She smiled gently, a sad understanding flickering across her face.

"Because it takes one to know one," she said softly.

Then she told me about her younger brother. They had been inseparable growing up, sharing secrets, dreams, and an unbreakable bond that she thought would last forever. But a misunderstanding – one of those stupid, preventable arguments that spiral out of control – had built a wall between them. Years passed with silence stretching between them, neither willing to be the first to reach out. And then, suddenly, he was gone. Not dead, but gone from her life in a way that felt just as permanent, just as devastating.

"He was my best friend," she said quietly, her voice thick with emotion. "When he left, it felt like something inside me broke. Like a piece of my soul had been ripped away. For a long time, I thought happiness wouldn't exist without him. I convinced myself that joy was something I'd never experience again, that I was condemned to live

in this perpetual state of grief and regret. But one day I realized – and this took me years to understand – people can leave, even if they promise you every single day that they won't. They still can. Life is unpredictable, and people are even more so. But they can't take our peace unless we let them. That's the power we still hold, even when everything else feels lost."

Her words found me exactly where I was, speaking directly to the hollow ache I'd been carrying.

That was one of the pivotal reasons I connected with her so deeply — her heartbreak was platonic too, just like mine. She understood the kind of pain that doesn't fit into society's definitions of grief. She listened to me and understood in a way most people in my life never could. Everyone else had kept saying, "But she wasn't your boyfriend," as if love only mattered when it was romantic. But she knew better. She knew the pain of losing someone who was your home, your comfort, your safe place — and that was enough.

Another thing about our conversation that struck me, that really resonated deep in my bones, was when she said, "Losing someone is still not a greater loss than losing your own self. After my brother left, I lost myself for a while. I became a shell, going through the motions but not really living. I forgot who I was before the loss defined me. But then, slowly, I found myself again and promised myself I would never let this happen again. People leaving or losing someone is not something in our control – no matter how tightly we try to hold on, we can't control the comings and goings of others. But losing ourselves? That is in our control. I lost the child in me for years until I found the child in me again, that sense of wonder and joy and spontaneity, the child that makes life worth living. I will never let myself lose that child again. Never."

She didn't fix anything with her words – grief doesn't work that way, I've learned. But she helped me see that healing was possible, that I wasn't destined to stay in this dark place forever.

My favorite part of my personality is the child in me, that playful, curious, hopeful part of my soul, a part of me that I enjoyed the most and something I have always loved about myself. It's the part that laughs without restraint, that finds beauty in small things, that believes in possibility. And if I truly loved something, why am I not trying to get something back that is mine and is actually in my control to bring back? Why was I allowing grief to steal what loss couldn't take unless I surrendered it?

The conversation changed my perspective entirely and became an integral part in my healing journey. It was the turning point, the moment when I stopped just surviving and started considering that maybe, just maybe, I could learn to live again.

FOUND

Healing wasn't instant. It came in waves. Some days, I was functional, fine—the routines of the world felt solid under my feet. But then a random trigger would hit, and the floor would drop out. I'd fall right back into the abyss.

There were nights I'd reach for my phone, I'd fight the urge, but eventually, I'd open the screen and type her name. I'd check her work pages, looking for the briefest glimpse of her or hear her voice in a video. It was my quiet way of keeping her close, because I couldn't talk to anyone about it — no one would understand.
Those moments gave me comfort, even if they hurt later.

But slowly, something changed. The shift wasn't a grand gesture; it was quiet, an almost stubborn commitment to my own stability. I began focusing on myself, on grounding the life she helped me build. I started journaling, less as an emotional purge and more as an attempt to self-diagnose and self-advise. The morning walks weren't escapes—they were mandatory steps to prove I could manage the day without her reassuring presence. These small, self-imposed rituals were acts of internal self-parenting. They were proof that I could create meaning and stability, even a tiny sliver, that existed outside the orbit of her absence. I was building a life, piece by piece, that didn't revolve around what was missing, but rather, one that relied on the lessons she had already imparted.

One night, the realization arrived silently. It had been weeks since I'd searched her name. Then months. I hadn't fought the urge; the urge simply hadn't appeared. And now, I look at the calendar and realize it's been nearly two years.

It's not because I stopped loving her, or because the memories faded. It's because I finally found peace in the love itself—a contained, beautiful legacy that I now carry forward, allowing the present to belong entirely to me, the person she helped me become.

Peace and Acceptance

I was grieving her — that's what it was all along.
And grief doesn't only visit after death; it lingers for the living too.
Death, paradoxically, can still bring some sort of forced acceptance. There is a brutal, final clarity to it: It wasn't in anyone's control, and there is absolutely no hope left to get the person back. But when someone you rely on simply leaves you—walks away, or cuts the connection—it becomes infinitely harder. You constantly want to reach out, to interrogate the silence for answers, to negotiate their return. The hope that maybe something will change, maybe they will come back. The questions and hope keep you up all night, crying and aching.
At first, I was trapped there, in denial. I'd tell myself she might reach out, that this cold silence was only temporary, a misunderstanding that would eventually thaw. But as time passed, acceptance came quietly—not

through the brutal act of forgetting the person, but through the difficult, patient work of remembering differently. I had to re-categorize the memories, moving them from the file labeled What I *Lost* to now called What I Was *Given*.

There's a line that always stays with me:
"Grief is all the love you still have, but no longer have a place to go."
That's exactly what it felt like — so much love, with nowhere to pour it.

Now, I still remember everything she ever told me. But instead of holding on to the pain, I hold on to the warmth — her laughter, her lessons, her advice, her guidance.

Even when I was hurting—when the lack of her presence—it was fundamentally rooted in love. And now, it's still love, but it has changed its form. It is softer, freed

from the demanding expectation of reciprocity, and intensely peaceful. I've accepted that I will always love her, even if I never see her again.
And if one day I do, that love will feel the same — quiet, steady, kind.
Because my love for her doesn't live in the past anymore.
It lives in peace.

I also learned a profound truth: you can always keep someone in your life by focusing on the positives they taught you, how they helped you, and what you loved about them. She is always going to be a part of my life because everything she's taught me as a mother figure stays with me every day of my life and still shapes me to be a better person. When I handle a difficult work situation with patience, that is her. When I give someone the same advice she once gave me, that is her. She is in my life through all the lessons, through the vivid memories of the laughter we shared, and in the quiet, steady discipline she instilled when I needed it. It is truly in my control to keep her alive within my actions and decisions, even if she is physically not present.

The loss broke me, but finding what I needed the most to find, *Myself*, bought me peace.

Blessing in Disguise

When I look back now, with a calmer heart and clearer mind, I realise that what once felt like the end of everything was actually the beginning of something far more meaningful.
Losing her felt unbearable at the time — it shattered me, shook the ground I stood on. But with distance, I see it differently now. It wasn't destruction; it was a necessary redirection.

Had I not gone through that heartbreak, I might never have found my purpose.
I was so emotionally anchored in her — so dependent on her presence, her guidance, her validation — that I

never paused to build those foundations within myself. I had made her my centre, my comfort, my reason. And when she left, that void forced me to face what I had been avoiding all along: *me.*

That heartbreak was my awakening.
It stripped away the illusion that my peace and happiness depended on anyone else. It pushed me to heal, to rebuild, and to finally discover that everything I had been seeking from her — comfort, direction, love, reassurance — had always existed within me.

She was my teacher, not just in love but in loss. Her absence became the silence where I finally heard my own voice again.
And now, when I think of her, I don't feel pain — I feel gratitude.
Because she wasn't my ending.
She was the turning point — the divine disruption that led me to my purpose, my healing, and my truth.
For that, I will always be grateful.

I only have love, respect, and the deepest gratitude for her — for the lessons, for the warmth, for the space she once held in my life.

I know now that love doesn't have to end with presence; it can continue in peace.

I will always hold that love with gentleness — not as a wound, but as a gift that helped me grow. It was, after all, a blessing in disguise.

(In the next chapter, we'll look at another illusion I once believed — that happiness could be bought, achieved, or earned. Because once I stopped depending on people for happiness, I realised I was still trying to buy it in different ways)

3
Borrowed Happiness

"I gave pieces of myself to everyone, thinking I was spreading love — until I realised I was slowly emptying my own cup."

For the longest time, I genuinely believed

happiness lived in the way people reacted to me — in their smiles, their thank-yous, their warmth, their appreciation. When someone appreciated something I did, I felt worthy.
When someone smiled because of me, I felt valuable.
And when someone needed me, I felt loved.

Gift-giving became my love language — not because I was materialistic, but because it gave me a sense of purpose.

I loved thinking of thoughtful things, planning surprises, creating moments that would make someone's eyes light up. And yes, those smiles did make me happy... but only for a moment.

The spark faded quickly. The joy didn't stay. The emptiness always returned.

I remember vividly the countless times I pushed myself beyond my limits — emotionally, mentally, financially — just to keep people happy.

And the truth was harsh:

I was thinking I am giving love. But I was actually borrowing happiness.

Borrowing it from the reactions of others.

Borrowing it every time someone said, "You're so thoughtful," or "No one does things like you."

Borrowing it every time I felt needed.

The joy I felt when doing something for someone else was transient, dissipating as quickly as it had come. My happiness was stitched together by everyone else's moods and reactions.

And that realisation broke me a little… but it also saved me.

This prompted me to embark on a journey of self-discovery and a quest to unravel the essence of genuine self-owned happiness.

"We cannot pour from an empty cup."
I always heard this phrase. But I never understood it — until I realised how empty my own cup had become.

Giving To Borrow Happiness

It took me a long time to see that my "acts of love" were often a way of avoiding my own emptiness. I was so used to focusing on other people's happiness that I forgot to nurture my own.

When people smiled at my efforts, I smiled too even if my heart felt hollow.

When they appreciated me, I felt seen even if I was falling apart inside.

But when someone was distant, unavailable, distracted, or less responsive…

my world would crash.

A delayed message, a short reply, someone being busy —

it had the power to change my entire day.

One unreturned text could ruin my mood.

One ignored gesture could make me question my worth.

One indifferent reaction could make me feel invisible.

That's when I understood something powerful:

True happiness doesn't depend on exchange.
It doesn't ask for a smile in return.
It doesn't wait for applause, recognition, or validation.

When we give from an empty place, we aren't giving —
We're trading.

Trading pieces of ourselves to feel valuable.
Trading energy for affection.
Trading effort for belonging.
Trading our emotional stability for temporary validation that disappears the moment people get busy, tired, distracted, or simply human.

And it is exhausting to live like that.

"You teach people how to love you by the way you love yourself."
— Rupi Kaur

I wasn't teaching people how to love me.

I was teaching them that I would give endlessly, without boundaries, without pause, without asking for anything in return.

Learning to Pour Back Into Myself

Healing didn't mean I stopped giving.
It meant I stopped giving to be chosen, giving to be seen, giving to feel enough.
When I started working on myself, I didn't stop giving — I just changed *why* I gave.
I started asking myself simple questions:
"Am I giving because I want to, or because I need to feel needed?"
"Am I sharing love, or am I trying to earn it?"
That's when everything began to shift.

I learned that giving doesn't have to come from exhaustion. It can come from abundance. From a place where you're already full — where sharing doesn't drain you, it expands you.

I started small, spending time with myself without guilt, doing things that made *me* feel alive, learning to sit with silence without needing to fill it.
And slowly, I began to refill my own cup.

And once I was fuller inside, I noticed something surprising:
I became less desperate for external reactions.
The joy that used to flicker only when someone smiled at me...
began to grow on its own.

Quietly.
Steadily.
Deeply.

It no longer felt borrowed.
It felt like mine.

> *"You owe yourself the love that you so freely give to others."*

True Happiness Is Not Transactional

Not only did I learn that true happiness is intrinsic, but I also discovered that when we place the responsibility for our happiness on others, we hand them our power.

And people — being human — will always drop it sometimes.

Not because they don't care.

But because they have their own lives, their own moods, their own battles, their own wounds.

Relying on others to make us happy sets unrealistic expectations and disappointment always follows when circumstances shift or people change. Expecting people to stay consistent is unfair.

Expecting them to meet needs we haven't even learned to meet within ourselves is unrealistic.

Happiness cannot be bought, earned, or gifted. When I embraced the truth that happiness is not transactional, everything changed.

I realised:

No one could give me happiness if I couldn't give it to myself

Approval isn't love

Validation isn't security

Attention isn't connection

And happiness isn't something to be *earned*

It's something to be *grown*.

Through self-awareness.
Through boundaries.
Through compassion for myself.
Through understanding that I deserve joy — not because someone gives it to me, but because I exist.

And for the first time, I wasn't chasing happiness.
I was living it — in stillness, in solitude, in peace.

Even when no one was watching...
I felt whole.

"The moment you stop seeking love outside yourself, you discover it was within you all along."

Closing Reflection

There's a quiet kind of peace that comes when you stop chasing borrowed happiness.
When you stop trying to fill your heart with echoes of other people's emotions and begin tending to your own.

The truth is, happiness borrowed will always fade but happiness cultivated within you becomes your constant companion.

So, before you pour into someone else's cup, pause for a moment.
Fill yours first.
Not out of selfishness, but out of love.

Because only when your cup overflows can your giving become genuine, not borrowed, not conditional — but whole.

4

The Illusion of Happiness

"Not every smile is born of joy, and not every Silence is sadness."

There's a strange pressure that comes with being human — an unspoken rule that we should always appear "fine," even when we're not.
Over time, I noticed how naturally we fall into it. Someone asks, *"How are you?"* and the response slips out without thought:
"I'm good."
Even on the days we feel far from it.

It made me wonder — when did "being okay" become a performance?

We grow up hearing things like "be positive," "don't be sad," "come on, cheer up," as if any feeling outside of happiness needs fixing. It conditions us to believe that happiness must always be visible, always present, always ready.

And so, instead of sharing what's real, we soften it.
We shrink it.
We hide it.

Not because we're dishonest, but because we've learned that honesty sometimes can be uncomfortable.
We fear being misunderstood.
We fear being judged as "too emotional" or "too sensitive."
We fear being seen in the moments when our emotions don't look polished or pretty.

I remember once coming across a line from Shakespeare that said, *"A man may smile and smile and be a villain."*

The irony hit me — because he wasn't talking about happiness at all, he was talking about how deceptive appearances can be.

And for the first time, I realised that even centuries ago, humans struggled with this same illusion:

that what we show the world is rarely what we are within.

And little by little, we learn something dangerous:

It is easier to appear happy than to explain why we're not.

That's how the illusion begins — not through big lies, but through tiny, everyday moments where we choose comfort over truth.
Not because we want to deceive anyone, but because we're still trying to understand our own feelings.

As I went deeper into my journey of understanding happiness, I realised something important:

We don't fake happiness because we are weak.
We do it because we're human.

We do it because life is loud and fast and demanding, and somewhere along the way, we began to believe that our emotions should never be inconvenient — not for others, not for ourselves.

But emotions don't disappear just because we soften them.
What we hide quietly stays with us loudly.

This chapter is not about the smile itself —
This chapter begins with the truth beneath everything:
The pressure to appear happy can be heavier than the sadness we're trying to hide.

And once I saw that, I realised happiness isn't just misunderstood — it's often mistaken altogether.

The Smiling Mask

We've all heard it—maybe from a stranger, a cheerful colleague, or a well-meaning relative: "Hey! Smile, be happy!"

It's what people say when they sense sadness, discomfort, or a moment of silence they can't quite understand. That pause, that hesitation in our expression, makes them uneasy. It's an unspoken demand for comfort. And usually, we comply. We reflexively pull the edges of our mouth up, we nod briskly, maybe even force out a loud, quick laugh to reassure *them*—and perhaps, deep down, to convince ourselves that we're okay, too.

But does a smiling face truly reflect happiness? Is joy something that can be captured and proven in a single expression?

If smile = happy, then why do I not feel the happiness within when I perform a smile?

I spent years perfecting that compliance. I learned to activate the mask the moment I stepped outside my front door. It wasn't just a friendly gesture; it was a necessary piece of social equipment.

I remember once having to attend a work event right after receiving truly devastating personal news. My mind was a blizzard of panic and grief, but my body went through the motions. Every time a new person approached, I had to physically stretch my face into that bright, unwavering smile.

think about it —

If I share a joke that makes you laugh in a moment like that, does that laughter mean you're truly happy? Or does it simply mean, for a brief, weightless moment, you forgot the heavy burden settled inside you?

So a smile is a façade?

We've been taught to equate genuine joy with visibility—with beaming smiles, loud laughter, and constant, bubbling excitement—as if those are the only acceptable languages happiness can speak. We assume that if someone is quiet, they must be miserable. If they aren't performing joy, they must be broken. But the truth is, those bright, public displays are often just the costumes happiness wears, not its quiet, steady essence.

"We wear smiles like armour, not because we're happy — but because it's safer than being seen."

The real exhaustion isn't in the sadness; it's in the performance. It's the constant mental calculation required to ensure your eyes don't betray the lie your mouth is telling. It's the fear of someone asking, *"Are you okay, really?"* and having to quickly formulate an easy, digestible answer.

The real question is: What happens the second the door closes and the mask slides off? What does happiness actually look like when no one is watching, and you finally grant yourself the permission to stop performing?

The Illusion

On my quest to find true happiness, I often found myself stuck on a single, nagging question: Why didn't outward expressions of joy—the smiles, the quick laughter—ever translate into a genuine, lasting peace within?

I started calling this "The Illusion of Happiness"—the deceptive appearance of smiling and laughing when, deep down, I felt nothing close to joy. It was a perfectly painted stage set where the lead actor (me) was internally collapsing.

We often hear the phrase, "Sad people are the ones who smile the most." This isn't just a cliché; it's a painful observation of reality. If smiles and laughter truly signify deep-seated happiness, then why are so many people who wear them still fighting silent battles inside? Shouldn't a wide, beaming smile mean we're okay? Shouldn't booming laughter mean we've finally healed? These questions haunted me because they were reflections of my own hypocrisy. I knew I was smiling hardest on the days I felt most lost.

I had to stop chasing the outward signs and start digging. I spent countless quiet moments reflecting—not distracting myself, but truly sitting—digging through layers of frantic emotion, trying to understand what happiness felt like beyond the surface performance.

This practice began with the hardest step: giving myself permission to simply feel. It meant sitting with thoughts of sadness, confusion, or disappointment without rushing to fix, distract, or suppress them. It felt like holding a painful, shivering animal in my lap. I allowed the anxiety to buzz in my chest and the confusion to cloud my mind, giving those difficult feelings their own voice, their own allotted time.

Somewhere along the way, I realized that true happiness had little to do with high-energy excitement or surface-level laughter. It wasn't the peak of the roller coaster.

It was peace.

It was stillness.

It was the quiet satisfaction that didn't need an audience—the kind that settles over you when your inner and outer self finally feel aligned and at ease. It felt like coming home after a long, exhausting journey and finally kicking off my shoes. I wasn't thrilled or ecstatic; I was simply *present* and *safe*.

"Happiness is not the absence of problems; it's the ability to deal with them."
— Steve Maraboli

That quote made sense to me only after I experienced the truth of it.
Because I realised happiness isn't the loud, sparkly emotion we've been taught to idolise.

It's not the butterflies in the stomach, not the constant laughter, not the Instagram-worthy moments.

It's the grounded feeling that remains even when life isn't perfect.
It's the inner steadiness that doesn't disappear when challenges appear.
It's the ability to sit with yourself — without fear, without masks — and still feel whole.

That's when it finally struck me:
Happiness isn't about feeling good all the time.
It's about feeling whole, even when life is far from perfect.

Behind the Smile

There was a time when I truly mastered the art of smiling through everything. It wasn't just a casual habit; it was a skill I honed. You could look at me at my lowest point and think, *She's fine. She's strong. She's got it completely together.*

And maybe that's exactly what I wanted you to think—maybe that performance was the only way I measured my worth. If I appear to be strong, then I must be strong.

Every "I'm fine" became a reflex, a line of code executed before my brain could even process the question. Every "Don't worry, I'm okay" was a calculated move—a simple, polite way to make others comfortable, even while I was quietly and systematically falling apart inside. I remember feeling like my body was a house with a huge, beautiful porch, while all the internal walls were crumbling to dust.

I kept up this intense, beautiful pretense because I thought that pretending would eventually *make* it true. At one point, I got so used to smiling that I began believing the performance myself. I never paused to reflect on whether that wide, steady smile came from true happiness or just ingrained habit. I just assumed that if I could hold it in place long enough, maybe the internal reality would finally match the external display.

I had become so good at pretending that the mask was no longer a disguise; it was simply my face.

And honestly, for a while, it worked. People stopped asking difficult follow-up questions. They took my answer at face value. Life went on, moving quickly and efficiently around my perfect, still performance.

But I didn't go on.

There's a strange, profound exhaustion that comes with pretending to be happy. It's a bone-deep weariness that no amount of sleep can fix, because the true source of the fatigue is mental. It's heavy—carrying a smile that doesn't belong to you, one that uses up every single ounce of your available emotional energy just to keep the corners lifted.

The greatest cost of the mask was the total lack of authenticity. Every forced smile felt like a debt I was running up against myself, borrowing from tomorrow's peace just to get through today's expectation.

"Sometimes pretending to be strong is the only way to survive — until one day, you realise you don't have to pretend anymore."

I used to think that if I kept showing up with a smile, the sadness would get tired and leave.
That if I ignored my heaviness long enough, it would eventually give up and fade away.

But emotions don't work that way.
They're patient.
They're persistent.
They sit quietly in the corners of your mind, waiting for the moment you're no longer distracted.

What we suppress doesn't disappear; it waits.
It waits for the silence.
It waits for the stillness.

It waits for the moment your mask slips — even for a second — so it can lean in and whisper:
"You still have to feel this."

And when it finally surfaces, it demands to be felt — completely.
All at once.
Without warning.
As if it's reclaiming the space you tried to deny it.

Behind the smile was where my real self lived — bruised, tired, unheard.
And learning to face that version of myself was the first step toward understanding what happiness actually is... and what it is not.

The Pressure to Be Happy

We live in a world that relentlessly glorifies positivity. From the slogans on our coffee mugs to the advice we receive when we're struggling, the message is uniform and pervasive: *look on the bright side*. We are taught from a young age that optimism is the default setting for a successful life, and anything less is a malfunction that needs to be fixed.

Scroll through social media, and you will see the evidence of this demand everywhere. We are inundated with endless highlight reels—smiling faces, perfect sunsets, career milestones, and curated success stories. We see the finished product, but never the messy process. We see the vacation, but not the stress of travel; the promotion, but not the burnout. Rarely do we see pain, confusion, or stillness in our feeds. Because we curate our lives for consumption, we edit out the shadows, leaving only the blinding light.

Consequently, we start believing that happiness is a constant state—something we must maintain to be seen as thriving, grateful, or emotionally "healthy." We internalize the idea that if we aren't radiating joy, we are somehow failing. We treat our emotions like a performance review, checking boxes to prove to the world (and ourselves) that we are okay. The pressure becomes a heavy cloak; we feel guilty for our sadness and ashamed of our anxiety, compounding our natural struggles with a layer of judgment.

We forget that it is only human to have bad days, quiet days, and days when breathing itself feels like the only progress we can make. The spectrum of human emotion is vast, yet we try to force ourselves into a single, narrow band of "happy." We deny ourselves the necessary seasons of winter—the dormancy, the grief, and the rest—that allow for eventual growth.
And yet, the world keeps telling us:

Smile.

Think positive.

Be grateful.

As if the complexity of human emotion can be fixed with a motivational quote.

The illusion isn't that happiness exists — of course it does.

The illusion is that it should exist **all the time**, without interruption, without fluctuation, without being touched by reality. We have bought into the myth of permanence, believing that once we achieve happiness, we are supposed to set up camp there and never leave. But emotions are weather, not geography. They pass through us; we do not live inside them.

"We think happiness is a destination, when it's really the courage to show up exactly as we are."
— Brené Brown

Life simply doesn't work in absolutes.
To expect constant happiness is to deny half of our reality.
Happiness isn't the absence of pain; it's the presence of meaning.
It's the ability to sit with discomfort and still know it doesn't define your entire existence.

It's the quiet understanding that heaviness is just a moment — not your identity.

Real resilience isn't about smiling through the storm or pretending the rain isn't cold.
It's about recognising your strength to endure it, and trusting that you'll find your way back to peace once it passes.
It's a quiet confidence, not a loud proclamation — the kind that whispers,
"I can survive this, even if today doesn't look pretty."

True happiness has nothing to prove.

It doesn't need to be loud or constant or Instagram-worthy.

It doesn't ask you to deny your pain or hide your humanity.

It simply asks for honesty — and the courage to feel what you feel without shame.

Learning to Be Real

There came a quiet turning point in my life when the weight of the mask simply became too heavy to carry. I realized that every time I hid my pain behind a reflexively polite smile, or answered "I'm fine" when my world was crumbling, I was betraying a small, vital part of myself. It was a betrayal of the inner child who didn't want to be "fixed"—the part of me that simply longed to be seen, heard, and understood in all my messiness.

So, I made a conscious choice to stop forcing myself to "be happy." I laid down the exhausting burden of maintaining an image. I stopped treating my emotions as problems to be solved and started treating them as visitors to be acknowledged. I allowed myself to just *be*.

The transition wasn't immediate, but it was liberating. Some days, "being" meant crying without guilt, letting the tears fall not as a sign of weakness, but as a necessary release of pressure. Some days, it meant choosing silence instead of filling the air with forced laughter or empty conversation. I learned that I didn't need to entertain others with my joy if I wasn't feeling it.

And then, slowly, the landscape shifted. Some days, it meant smiling again. But this time, the smile wasn't plastered on to make others comfortable; it was unbidden. It reached my eyes. It was real.

That is when I began to truly understand the profound difference between *performing* happiness and *experiencing* it. Performing is a transaction; it drains you because it requires constant energy to keep the facade from cracking. Experiencing happiness is restorative; it fills you up from the inside out.

I learned that authentic happiness isn't loud. It doesn't need to announce itself with fanfare, post about itself for likes, or seek external validation to prove it exists.

Instead, it is quiet, grounded, and deeply personal. It is the feeling of a deep exhale, a warm cup of tea, or a moment of clarity. It is sturdy enough to handle the truth of life. It is the kind of happiness that can coexist with sadness—because you have learned to hold both ends of the spectrum without shame. You no longer shame yourself for feeling too much or too little.

You learn to hold every emotion with softness.

> *"The truest form of happiness is the one that asks nothing of you but honesty."*

The Truth Beneath the Illusion

The illusion of happiness tells us we must always be okay.
It whispers that anything less than cheerful means something is wrong with us — that sadness is a failure, that heaviness is weakness, that vulnerability makes us difficult to love.

But real happiness doesn't demand perfection.
It doesn't ask you to deny your humanity.

It doesn't require you to trim your emotions into neat, acceptable shapes.
Real happiness lives comfortably beside imperfection — not in spite of it, but *with* it.
Because the truth is this:
You can feel joy and grief in the same breath.

There came a point in my journey where I finally stopped chasing the idea that happiness must be constant, uninterrupted, and spotless.
I realised that the more I tried to force happiness into a permanent state, the more it slipped through my fingers.
It's like trying to grip water — the tighter you hold, the more it escapes.

So I stopped fighting my emotions.
I stopped rushing myself into feeling "better."
I stopped trying to curate my inner world into something presentable.

And strangely, that's when peace began to grow.

Not because life suddenly became perfect — far from it. But because I stopped resisting what was real.

I learned that contentment isn't found in avoiding discomfort, but in allowing it. In saying, *"Yes, this hurts… and that's okay."*
When I made space for all my emotions instead of only the pleasant ones, happiness stopped feeling like a pursuit and started feeling like a presence.

Now, when someone says, "Smile, be happy," I smile — not because I'm expected to, not because it's polite, and not because I'm hiding.
I smile when I genuinely feel it, when it rises naturally from a place of alignment and truth.
And some days, I don't smile at all.
And that's okay too.

Because I no longer measure my worth by how "together" I appear.

I no longer mistake silence for sadness or tears for weakness.

I no longer see happiness as a performance I have to maintain.

The illusion of happiness is exhausting — a constant performance, a weight you carry on your face.

But the truth of happiness —
the soft, imperfect, quiet kind —
is freedom.

It's the freedom to be honest.
The freedom to feel.
The freedom to be fully human.

And that freedom is happiness in its purest form.

Closing Reflection

Happiness is not a performance; it's a presence.
It's not about looking okay — it's about being honest about where you are.

Sometimes happiness is a laugh that escapes between tears.
Sometimes it's a deep breath after a long cry.
And sometimes, it's simply the peace of saying,
"I'm not okay today, but I know I will be."

Because the illusion fades.
But the truth stays.

5

When Purpose Found Me

"What you seek is seeking you." - Rumi

There was a time when I woke up every morning and simply went through the motions—shower, coffee, commute, work, eat, repeat. I was following a routine so strictly that I had stopped noticing the days passing. On paper, life was fine. I was functioning. I was ticking all the boxes of what a "good life" was supposed to look like.

I felt like the living embodiment of that old Benjamin Franklin quote: *"Many people die at twenty-five and aren't buried until they are seventy-five."*

I wasn't dead, obviously, but I wasn't fully alive either. Inside, something was missing.

It wasn't sadness—I had known sadness before, and I knew how heavy that felt. This was different. It was quieter. It was an emptiness that whispered rather than screamed.It was a low-level hum in the back of my mind, feeling that I was just passing time rather than actually living it. A quiet knowing that there must be more to life than just paying bills and waiting for the weekend.

I remember sitting on the edge of my bed one evening, completely exhausted after another long day. I looked around my room. I had stability. I had people who loved me. I had the things I thought I wanted. Yet, I felt nothing.

That night, it hit me: I had built a life around *doing*, but not around *meaning*.

I had fallen into the trap of the "human doing" rather than the "human being." For so long, I poured myself into people, into work, into distractions—anything that made me feel useful. I thought that if I kept moving, the emptiness wouldn't catch up to me.

Socrates once warned to *"beware the barrenness of a busy life,"* and I finally understood what he meant. You can be busy every second of the day and still be empty.

I realized then that usefulness and fulfillment are not the same.

You can spend your whole life giving, fixing, and working. You can be the most reliable person in the room. But you can still feel hollow if that giving doesn't come from a place of real purpose.

As the philosopher Howard Thurman said: *"Don't ask what the world needs. Ask what makes you come alive, and go do that. Because what the world needs is people who have come alive."*

I had spent so much time asking what the world needed from me that I had forgotten to ask what made me come alive.

Purpose found me when I finally sat in that uncomfortable space and asked myself what *I* needed, what lit me up, what made me feel alive beyond responsibility, beyond identity, beyond habit.

And that was the beginning.

Not of becoming someone new,

but of finally returning to myself.

The Whisper of Meaning

After losing someone I considered my foundation, The silence that followed was unbearable. It wasn't a peaceful quiet; it was a heavy, suffocating absence. I tried to fill it with noise, with busyness, with anything to avoid facing the void. But eventually, when the distractions ran out, I had to sit in it.

And in that silence, I heard something new: a whisper.

A whisper that didn't give me answers, but forced me to ask the questions I had spent years avoiding.

Who am I without the people I depend on?
What remains of me when the comforting presence I

built myself around disappears?

What gives my life meaning beyond others — beyond attachment, beyond giving, beyond roles I've always played?

What makes me feel alive... not for someone else, but for me?

It was a terrifying confrontation. As the psychologist Carl Jung once said, *"The privilege of a lifetime is to become who you truly are."* I realized I had spent so much time being who I was to *them*, I had forgotten who I was to *me*.

It's strange how heartbreak can sometimes become the door to awakening. We tend to think of pain as something that only takes away, but it also clears the ground.

It wasn't until everything I leaned on collapsed that I realised how little of myself I had truly explored.
Losing her didn't just hurt —
It stripped me bare enough to finally see myself.

As Leonard Cohen famously wrote: *"There is a crack in everything. That's how the light gets in."*

I had to break to let the light in.

And beneath all the noise, beneath the grief and the confusion, I found something familiar. I found the same thing I had as a child—empathy, curiosity, connection.
The part of me that watched people closely — not to judge, but to understand.
The part that always wanted to soothe pain, even when I didn't know how to soothe my own.
The part that listened without needing to speak.
The part that felt deeply — sometimes too deeply — but never stopped feeling.

That was the whisper.

A voice that had always been there but was drowned out by life, by noise, by roles, by expectations, by heartbreaks, and by my own distractions.

It said:

"You were made for meaning."
"You were made to understand people."
"You were made to heal — yourself and others."

Not loudly.

Not urgently.

But consistently.

Gently.

Patiently.

And for the first time, I didn't run from it.

I listened.

And that listening — that moment of stillness, vulnerability, and truth — became the beginning of everything that followed.

I was finally meeting myself again.

From Giving to Growing

For as long as I can remember, I've always carried a soft instinct to be there for people. In quiet, subtle moments that often go unnoticed. I was the person friends called when they needed to talk. The one who listened without rushing, without judging, without trying to fix things too quickly. Even as a teenager, adults in my family would talk to me as if I carried an understanding beyond my years.

I never thought much of it then. It felt natural—almost second nature.

But when I began truly reflecting on my life, especially after everything I had lost and rebuilt, I realized something deeper: I wasn't drawn to people's stories by accident.

I wasn't patient or understanding because I was trying to impress anyone. There was something in me—empathy, intuition, connection—that unfolded effortlessly every time someone trusted me with their pain or their truth.

I realised that I felt most alive in those moments.
Not when I was achieving something.
Not when I was ticking off errands or chasing goals.

But when I was sitting with another human being in their rawness — giving them space to breathe, feel, and be seen.

It wasn't about being a "strong friend."
It wasn't about being available.
It wasn't even about helping, in the traditional sense.

It was about **connection**.It was about **presence**. It was about understanding people in ways words couldn't fully explain.

That realisation changed everything.

I noticed a pattern — one that had followed me throughout my entire life:
I was happiest when I was holding space for others.
I found fulfilment not in being needed, but in being trusted.
Not in fixing things, but in witnessing someone's growth and knowing my presence gave them courage.

And slowly, I began to ask myself:

What if this wasn't just a trait?
What if this was my calling?

What if the way I listened, the way people naturally opened up to me, the way I felt peace when I was helping someone understand their own emotions, wasn't random at all?

What if purpose wasn't something I had to chase—but something that had been waiting patiently for me to turn inward?

For the first time in my life, the question didn't feel overwhelming. It felt right. Aligned. Like finally recognizing a voice that had always been mine, just drowned by noise, heartbreak, and self-doubt.

In that moment, it became clear:

I wasn't just meant to feel deeply. I was meant to help others feel deeply too. I wasn't just meant to comfort. I was meant to guide. I wasn't just meant to listen. I was meant to heal.

And in that realization, my journey shifted—from simply giving pieces of myself away to growing into the person I was always meant to be.

The Calling Becomes Clear

Purpose doesn't always announce itself dramatically. Sometimes, it arrives gently — in the middle of an ordinary day, when you're tired of pretending and ready to feel again. For me, that moment came when I was volunteering. I remember sitting beside a woman who had just gathered the courage to speak about her struggles. Her voice trembled. Her hands fidgeted. She was holding on to so much, yet trying so hard to hold herself together.

I didn't say much.
I didn't have a perfect answer.
I didn't try to fix her story or make her pain look prettier.

I just… listened.

Truly listened — with the kind of attention that comes from the heart, not from a script.
And when she finished speaking, she looked at me with this small, fragile smile and whispered:

"You made me feel like I'm not broken."

Something shifted inside me in that exact moment — like a lock clicking open after years of being jammed.

Her words didn't flatter me; they awakened me.
They didn't inflate my ego; they grounded me.
It felt as if a part of me — the part I had buried under heartbreak, confusion, and emotional dependence — quietly rose to the surface and whispered back:

"This is who you are."

That night, I cried.
Not because I was hurting,
but because for the first time in a very long time, I felt *connected* —
not to a person,

not to an attachment,
not to temporary happiness…

…but to a **purpose**.

"The purpose of human life is to serve, and to show compassion and the will to help others."

– Albert Schweitzer

The Decision That Changed Everything

Even as a teenager, I was the person people came to.
Not because I had the answers — but because I listened. My aunties would sit with me for hours, sharing their stories, confusions, fears, and heartbreaks. They never spoke to me like I was a child; they spoke to me like someone who understood — someone who could hold space for their emotions without judgment.

My friends were the same.
They would call me, not for solutions but for comfort — because they knew I would show up with empathy, with

presence, with the kind of understanding that made people feel less alone.

I didn't realise it then, but I was practising counselling long before I had a title for it.

As I grew older, this pattern only deepened.

People gravitated toward me with their pain, their stories, their hopes.

It wasn't something I forced — it was something that flowed.

And the more it happened, the more I began to recognise that this wasn't just "being a good listener."

It was a gift.

It was a calling.

It was the part of me that had always been there, quietly shaping who I was becoming.

So when life finally pushed me into the direction of counselling, it did not surprise me. It did not confuse me. It clarified me.

I took that leap — the leap that would change everything.

I enrolled. I studied. I worked.
I doubted myself on some days, but on most days, I grew.
And somewhere between the lectures, the assignments, the late-night reflections, and the endless journaling, something beautiful happened:

I began to recognise *myself* again.

Not a new version of me — but the real one.
The one that was buried under people-pleasing, self-doubt, and borrowed happiness. The one I had forgotten because I had spent so long trying to be strong for others.

So when I decided to pursue counselling and life coaching, I knew this is what I was meant to do. I knew this is what came naturally to me—the desire to help others heal and channel it into a purpose-driven life.

It didn't surprise anyone who knew me. They would often say, *"Michelle, this suits you perfectly."* And they were right. I didn't choose counselling because I needed to find myself. I chose it because, through the practice of it, I could *be myself*.

Counselling didn't just give me a career.
It gave my compassion a direction.
It gave my empathy a purpose.
It turned my pain into understanding, my heartbreak into insight, and my curiosity into connection.

During that crucial time, I remember reading Viktor Frankl's *Man's Search for Meaning*, and one line stayed with me forever, grounding every moment of difficulty:

> *"Those who have a 'why' to live, can bear almost any 'how.'"*

That line became my anchor — because suddenly, everything I had been through made sense.

The heartbreak, the loneliness, the emptiness, the searching — they weren't punishments.
They were prepatory.
They brought me to my *why*.

And once I found my *why*, everything else — the "how," the "when," the "where" — started to fall into place.

Counselling became the perfect bridge between my heart and my purpose — a space where my empathy could transform into empowerment, where understanding could turn into healing, and where I could finally live a life that aligned with my soul.

"Purpose doesn't arrive as a surprise. It unfolds like a memory—something your soul always knew."

Becoming the Purpose

When I began practising, I thought I was stepping into this work to help others heal.
And I was. But what I didn't realise at the time was that I was healing too; quietly, gently, and almost unknowingly.

Every client who sat across from me carried a world within them; fears, heartbreaks, confusions, hopes they barely knew how to articulate. And as they unfolded their stories, something inside me began unfolding too.

There is something profoundly sacred about witnessing someone's vulnerability.
The way their pain and hope coexist.
The way they still show up, even when life has bruised them.
The way strength hides inside the most fragile moments.

Each session became a mirror — one that reflected not only their journey, but mine.

I saw my own wounds in their words.
I recognised my past in their fears.
I heard echoes of my younger self in the questions they asked.
And with every insight they gained, I felt something inside me soften, shift, and settle.

Healing, I realised, isn't a straight line.
It isn't a neat before-and-after moment.
It's layered.
Cyclical.
Human.
Some days you feel whole, and other days you're reminded of old wounds you thought were closed — but somehow, you're stronger in revisiting them.

There were moments in sessions where a client would say something that pierced through me, not as pain, but as truth.
A truth I needed to hear too.
A truth I didn't know I was ready for.

Helping others find their light helped me recognise my own.

I learned that purpose isn't just about what you do, it's about what it awakens in you.
My purpose wasn't only to guide others; it was to grow with them.
To sit in the quiet bravery of their stories and realise I, too, had survived so much.
I, too, had rebuilt.
I, too, had risen.

And somewhere along the way, something beautiful happened:

I stopped just *doing* the work — I became it.

Counselling stopped feeling like a career choice and began feeling like a homecoming.
It felt like the universe had woven all my heartbreaks, all my lessons, all my empathy into one path — and that path was asking me not just to walk it, but to *embody* it.

"When you help others heal, you end up healing yourself."

I used to think the purpose was something you found. But now I know —

purpose is something you become.

The Peace of Alignment

Now, when I look back at my journey, I no longer see a straight path—I see a necessary, chaotic series of moments that demanded I pause, break, and rebuild. Each painful moment wasn't a mistake; it was a fundamental requirement, guiding me closer to who I was meant to be.

Purpose didn't find me all at once. It arrived through heartbreak, through silence, through surrender. It found me when I stopped asking, *"What do I want from life?"* and started asking, *"What does life want from me?"*

And the answer was simple: to serve, to heal, to grow. Not just others — but myself, too.

And today, when I sit with a client, when I listen to a trembling voice trying to find its strength, when I witness someone's courage unfold in real time — I feel that peace in my bones.

This is where I was meant to be.
This is what life wanted from me.
This is the alignment I spent years searching for, without even realising it.
Purpose isn't a destination.
It's returning — back to yourself.

A Note to You, Reader

If you're reading this and still searching for your purpose — breathe. It's okay not to know yet.
You don't have to chase it; you just have to become still enough. Purpose isn't something you chase like a finish line — it's something you grow into.

Your purpose isn't hiding from you. It's waiting for you to notice it, in the subtle, almost invisible moments that make your heart stir without warning. Life reveals things when you're ready to receive them not when you're impatient to find them.

Purpose doesn't always roar into your life. Sometimes, it whispers.
And when you finally hear it, you'll know — because it will feel like *coming home.*

> *"Purpose unfolds in the space between who you were and who you're becoming."*

6

The If And When Trap

"We spend half our lives waiting for happiness to arrive, never realising it has been softly knocking all along — right here, in the now."

We humans have this strange habit — we keep postponing happiness. We treat joy like a reward that must be earned, usually by meeting some arbitrary future condition. We tell ourselves things like,, *"I'll be happy **if** this happens,"* or *"I'll be happy **when** I get there."*
It becomes a silent, automatic pattern we don't even realize we're repeating. It's like we've

signed a contract with ourselves: joy can only be experienced in the future tense.

But what about now?
What about this very moment that we're living?
Why do we so often skip over it, as if it's not worthy of happiness yet?

We think joy will arrive with a title, a relationship, a dream house, a milestone — something that validates that we've "made it."
And yet, each time we get there, the excitement fades, the satisfaction slips away, the moment we once prayed for becomes another item we silently move past. And suddenly, there's another "if" and another "when" waiting in line.
It's almost as if happiness keeps moving one step ahead of us, teasing us like a mirage in the desert — visible, close, but never quite within reach.

We spend so much time preparing for tomorrow that we forget how to live today.

"There is no way to happiness—happiness is the way."

— Thich Nhat Hanh

The Mirage of Tomorrow

It's comforting to believe that the future will fix everything.

That when life slows down, when we finally have enough — enough love, money, peace, or clarity — then we'll be happy.

It's a quiet lie we tell ourselves to make the chaos of the present feel more bearable.

I used to think like that too, not because I was ungrateful for what I had, but because that's the script we're handed. We're taught to chase milestones: finish school, get the demanding job, find a partner, and build a secure home. The promise is that somewhere along that checklist, happiness will be waiting.

But no one tells you what happens when you reach all those milestones and still feel something missing.

The truth is, that promised future is a mirage. It's an illusion because the future itself is not in our hands.

The future is just an idea—a thought decorated with hopes and plans.

I too treated it like a bank account for joy, constantly making deposits of patience and hardship, certain I'd make a massive withdrawal later.

But the truth is the only thing we truly hold is this moment.

Right now — as you're reading this, as I'm writing this.

But chasing happiness in "someday" is like running on a treadmill — you get exhausted, but you never move forward.

That's when it hit me — maybe happiness was never hiding in the next big thing.

Maybe it was quietly sitting beside me the whole time, waiting for me to stop running long enough to notice it.

The Only Time That Exists

The day this truth really sank in, something shifted inside me.

I realised that we never truly live in the past or the future — we only ever live in today.

Every yesterday I regretfully missed was once a today I took for granted. Every tomorrow I long for, will arrive disguised as another ordinary today. It's always *now*. That's the only time life ever gives us.

I begin to realise something unsettling —
The future is not a cure.
It is not a magical place where happiness blooms simply because time has passed.

The future is just a concept — a canvas we fill with our hopes, fears, and assumptions.

And if happiness doesn't happen here — in this breath, in this version of you — what makes you think it will magically appear somewhere else?

I stopped holding my peace hostage to a version of myself that didn't exist yet. I stopped waiting for clarity, love, success, or calm to feel grateful. Because I understood the future isn't promised, and the past is gone.

What I have, what you have, is this.

This ordinary moment.

This sip of tea, this ray of sunlight, this quiet breath.

This is life.

And this is where happiness lives.

Now, whenever my mind wanders into the anxious territory of "what if" or the restless longing of "one day," I remind myself gently:

The only time that ever truly exists is today—and I don't want to miss it while it's still here.

This final surrender to the present was the destination I had been searching for all along. It wasn't a place; it was a state of being.

Learning to Live in the Now

After realising the illusory nature of the "If and When Trap", I wanted to understand **How do you actually live in the "now"?**

It sounds poetic, almost obvious — "be present," "live in the moment," "stay grounded."
But *how*.
With a mind that drifts into the past without permission, or leaps anxiously into the future even when nothing has happened yet.

So I began searching — not out of desperation, but out of curiosity.

I wanted to understand what it meant to belong to the moment instead of constantly running from it.

One of the first teachings that found me during this time was Viktor Frankl's reflections in *Man's Search for Meaning*.

Frankl didn't talk about happiness in the way most books do — he didn't promise steps, strategies, or simple solutions.

Instead, he offered something far more profound:

Even in the most unbearable conditions, meaning — not pleasure or excitement — is what sustains us.

His words reminded me that no matter what life gives or takes away, the *way we interpret* that experience shapes everything.

Happiness isn't a result of circumstances; it's a result of perspective.

Two people can go through the same storm, but the one who looks for meaning will walk out stronger.

Frankl's message became an anchor for me — not because my life mirrored his suffering, but because his truth applied universally:

We cannot always control our life, but we can choose how we meet it.

Around the same time, I stumbled upon mindfulness — a word I had heard a thousand times but never truly understood.
I assumed mindfulness meant sitting silently and trying not to think, but it was the opposite.
It was about noticing.
Allowing.
Observing without judgement.

Mindfulness taught me that the present moment isn't something we reach — it's something we return to.

At first, I didn't even realise how disconnected I had been.
I wasn't living days; I was getting through them.
I wasn't experiencing moments; I was rushing past them.

But slowly, through practice, I became aware of things I had ignored for years —
the warmth of morning sunlight gently pouring into my room,
the way the air smelled after rain,
the quiet rhythm of my own breathing when I stopped long enough to notice it.

These tiny, ordinary details started to feel like small invitations back into my body, back into my life. Mindfulness wasn't "positive thinking" — it was honest thinking.

It taught me that emotions don't need to be fixed or hurried out the door.
They need to be felt.
Acknowledged.
Trusted.

And strangely, when I finally allowed myself to feel them without resistance, they passed through me with more ease. What mindfulness ultimately gave me was freedom — not from life, but from my own mind's habit of running away from the present.

And in that stillness, I learned something life-altering:

Happiness isn't found by escaping discomfort.
Happiness is found by meeting reality exactly where it is —
and still choosing peace within it.

Closing Reflection

I used to think happiness was waiting for me somewhere down the road.

Now I know it's right here — in the quiet rhythm of an ordinary day.

The future will always be uncertain, but the present is something I can hold, feel, and live in.

So I choose to be here — not waiting, not chasing, just being.

Because if happiness is anywhere at all,

it's in this very breath.

And it's enough.

> *"If you keep waiting for happiness to arrive, you'll miss the quiet moments where it's been living all along."*

7

Beyond Comparison

"Happiness loses its purity the moment it's measured against another's life."

A Shout-Out to My Roots

Before I begin this chapter, I want to give a heartfelt shout-out to my parents. They raised me with gratitude in my heart and peace in my mind and most importantly, they never taught me to measure my worth through comparison.

I was raised in a middle class family, we were 6 people living in a 2 bedroom home, we in fact never even had a car but just the way my parents raised us we never felt we lacked anything or we were "not rich". In our home, contentment wasn't something spoken about — it was something lived.

I grew up watching them celebrate what we had, however little or much it was, without glancing sideways to see who had more. They taught me to appreciate my blessings quietly, to clap for others loudly, and to stay grounded in my own world without needing to compete with anyone.

And I am endlessly thankful for that foundation.

But through my own journey — and especially through watching the people I love and deeply care about, lose their spark, their joy, their peace — all because of comparison.

Friends, family, even clients I've worked with — people who had beautiful lives, yet couldn't see their own light because they were too busy noticing someone else's shine.

It became a second-hand lesson for me; one that left a deep mark. I didn't have to go through the pain of comparison personally to understand its destructive power; witnessing it was enough.

I saw how comparison quietly chips away at happiness, little by little. It doesn't storm in — it whispers. It convinces you that your story isn't enough, your pace isn't right, your happiness isn't valid unless it mirrors someone else's.

And while I've always been someone who finds happiness in what I have, one conversation with a friend changed everything for me.

It became the reason this chapter was birthed — a reminder that even when we think we're immune, life has a way of holding up a mirror and showing us lessons we didn't know we needed.

The Thief Of Joy

It's strange how something as simple as a conversation can shake your entire perspective. I remember the day, as I sat listening to a friend, I didn't realize that a casual chat would become one of the most important lessons of my life.

She began comparing her life to others—their milestones, their timelines, their successes. I stayed quiet, listening, but somewhere in between her words, something unsettling started stirring in me. Without realizing it, my own mind began constructing a silent comparison chart. It wasn't plotting against her, but against myself.

And in that precise, uncomfortable moment, I caught myself.

I remember thinking, "Wait! what am I doing?"

It was almost unsettling how easily I slipped into that mindset—one I had always prided myself on avoiding due to my strong upbringing. I had always been grounded in gratitude, but that moment made me realize just how contagious comparison could be. Even if you are secure in who you are, someone else's dissatisfaction, or even just their focus on external metrics, can quietly plant tiny, toxic seeds of self-doubt in you if you're not careful.

That single moment became a mirror, showing me how fragile joy can be when you let the world, or even someone else's internal battle, set your standards.

I shook the thought off, but the feeling lingered. It didn't disappear, but it made me more aware, more intentional about guarding my inner world.

From that day on, I made it a deliberate practice to notice when those little comparisons tried to creep in and to gently remind myself that my story isn't supposed to look like anyone else's. My pace is my pace. My journey is entirely my own.

This experience made me realize how easy it is to lose joy not because of what we genuinely lack, but because of what we *think* we're supposed to have, based on a faulty external rubric.

Comparison doesn't always come with bitterness or obvious jealousy. Sometimes, it disguises itself as harmless observation, as necessary professional benchmarking, or as simple curiosity. But the internal shift is instantaneous: the moment you start wondering, *Why not me?* or *When will it be my turn?* joy begins to slip quietly out of your hands.

That's when I truly understood why they call comparison *"the thief of joy."*

Because it doesn't come screaming, it whispers. And before you know it, it convinces you that your blessings are too small, your timeline is too slow, and your unique story is too simple.

But joy isn't found in someone else's timeline—it's found in your own presence. That day, through that simple conversation, I learned that contentment isn't something you wait to feel once everything looks perfect.

It's something you protect, nurture, and choose—every single day.

The Balance Within

There's a delicate balance between being inspired by others and being consumed by comparison.

Inspiration uplifts you—comparison drains you..
The difference lies in your intention.

When I began appreciating others without questioning my own worth, I realised that happiness doesn't shrink when it's shared — it expands.

That balance didn't come overnight.

There were still days when I found myself slipping — scrolling through social media, noticing someone else's milestone, feeling that quiet tug inside that whispered, "You should be there by now." It was never loud or cruel, just a soft nudge, barely noticeable unless I paid attention.

But each time it happened, I caught that thought a little faster.
Each time, I reminded myself that I'm exactly where I'm

meant to be — not ahead, not behind, simply *here*, on my own timeline.

And that reminder became a practice.
A discipline.
A form of self-love.

Peace, I learned, is not the absence of comparison — it's the awareness of when it tries to creep in, and the strength to gently let it go before it plants itself inside you.

It's understanding that being inspired by someone else's journey doesn't mean you have to abandon your own. Inspiration is expansive — it makes you look inward and ask, *"How can I grow?"* Comparison shrinks you — it makes you look outward and ask, *"Why am I not there?"*

One gives you wings.
The other clips them.

And that, I learned, is the balance we spend our whole lives trying to find — the balance between appreciating the beauty around us and never forgetting the beauty within us.

Closing Reflection

That single conversation reminded me how delicate joy truly is, how it can slip away, not because life changes, but because our focus does.

Since that day, I've learned to protect my peace the way one guards something sacred.

Comparison will always try to find its way in — through words, through screens, through silence — but awareness is the shield that keeps it from settling.

Now, when I catch myself drifting into "why not me," I pause and smile.

Because I know — my path, my timing, my story — are mine alone.

8
Searching Happiness, Finding Contentment.

"Happiness is a visitor; contentment is home."

We often use happiness and contentment

interchangeably, as if they mean the same thing.

But through my journey — through heartbreak, silence, stillness, and rediscovery I realised that while they may walk side by side, they are not the same. Not even close.

Happiness is often loud.
It arrives with laughter, excitement, surprises,

celebrations, and those beautiful highs that make life feel warm and vibrant. It's the kind of emotion that sparkles — one you can see, hear, touch, and recognise instantly.

Contentment... contentment is different.
Contentment doesn't announce itself.
It doesn't make noise.
It doesn't need to be seen.

Contentment is quiet — the kind of quiet that settles gently in your chest.
It's the peace that stays after the excitement fades.
It's the gratitude that lingers long after the moment has passed.
It's the acceptance of what *is*, not what *could be*.

For the longest time, I confused the two. I thought if I was happy, I must be content.
But the truth revealed itself slowly — the first time happiness left and the emptiness returned. The first time the laughter faded, yet the restlessness remained.

The first time I noticed that even in moments of joy, something inside me still felt unsettled.

That's when I realised:
Happiness is a moment.
Contentment is a state.

Happiness is the spark.
Contentment is the flame that keeps burning.

Happiness comes and goes like a guest — knocking, entering, staying briefly, and then leaving, sometimes without warning.
Contentment is a home you build slowly, day by day, brick by brick — through awareness, acceptance, and inner peace. It's the place you return to when the world becomes loud, when people leave, when life shakes you.

It is the quiet hum beneath the noise of life.
The gentle grounding of your soul.
The soft, steady "I am okay," even on the days when happiness feels far away.

Happiness colours moments.
Contentment colours life.

And once I understood this, my entire definition of joy changed.
I stopped chasing moments.
And I started building a home within myself.

> *"Happiness is a moment we feel; contentment is the life we choose."*

The Difference We Often Miss

For a while, I believed happiness was the ultimate goal. That's what the world teaches us — to chase highs, to celebrate only the exciting parts, to collect smiles as proof of a good life. But the older I grew, the more I noticed how happiness demands a reason, while contentment doesn't.

Contentment doesn't need a "why." It just is.

There was a morning I remember vividly — nothing remarkable happened. No milestones, no big plans. I was just sitting on my balcony, with a cup of coffee, watching sunlight spill gently across the table. And for a fleeting second, I realised, It wasn't happiness. Happiness was what I felt when I celebrated birthdays, achieved goals, or laughed until I cried with friends.

This was different.

This was softer.

It was peace — unshaken, quiet, yet deeply fulfilling.

In that moment I was at peace without dependency on anyone, without doing something for someone, without loud love, without anything but just *me*. That's when it hit me — this is what contentment feels like. It doesn't rush, it doesn't demand attention. It simply is.

And that was enough.

That's the difference I want people to see — happiness is reactive; contentment is reflective.

Happiness says, "This moment makes me feel good."

Contentment says, "I am grateful for this moment — even if it's not perfect."

Michael A. Singer wrote in his book — *The Untethered Soul*, "You're not supposed to be happy all the time. You're supposed to be at peace." When I first read that, it felt like someone had put into words what I had been feeling.. Because that's exactly it; happiness visits when peace opens the door, but contentment is what keeps it from leaving.

I think the beauty of contentment is that it doesn't deny sadness. It doesn't silence longing. It simply creates space for them to exist without chaos. You can be content and still want more. You can be content and still have dreams unfulfilled. The difference is — you're not depending on their fulfilment to feel whole.

In many ways, contentment is the most radical form of self-acceptance. It's saying, "Even if nothing changes, I can still be at peace right here."

And that, to me, is the truest form of happiness there is.

The Lantern and the Flame

I like to think of happiness as a **flame**—bright, warm, and beautiful, but inherently fragile. It naturally glows when things go right, when people are kind, when life feels vibrant and good.

But that flame can also fade quickly. One bad day, one harsh word, one unexpected change in the wind, and it starts to shake, dim, or risk going out completely.

That's when I realized something deeper: we all need a lantern.

Contentment is that **lantern.** It is the durable structure that holds the flame steady when the winds of life blow too hard, when the external world becomes chaotic, or when circumstances change rapidly.

When you have contentment, your peace isn't controlled by the world around you. You're not depending on everything to go perfectly just to feel okay inside. You stop making the external conditions responsible for your internal state.

The glass and metal of that lantern are built from:

- **Gratitude:** Acknowledging the light you already possess.
- **Self-Awareness:** Noticing the winds (thoughts/emotions) without becoming the wind.
- **Acceptance:** Trusting the stability of the structure, regardless of the storm.

Because when your happiness (the flame) is protected by contentment (the lantern), the light doesn't go out.

It might shrink.
It might soften.
It might flicker on windy days.

But it stays.

The light remains.

The warmth remains.

You remain.

And that warmth — is yours to keep.

A flame the world didn't give you, and therefore, cannot take away.

What I Know Now

I used to chase happiness like it was something I could hold, but life kept reminding me that it was never meant to be caught. It was meant to be felt, to pass through, to remind us of what matters before moving on.

Contentment, though — that's what I learned to build, through gratitude, awareness, and acceptance. It became my steady companion in a world that never stops moving.

Now, when I find myself smiling, it isn't because everything is perfect. It's because I've made peace with imperfection.

It's because I've learned that joy doesn't always roar; sometimes, it hums quietly beneath the noise of life.

And in that stillness — in search of happiness, I found contentment.

Closing Reflection

If happiness is a feeling, then contentment is knowing.

It's the moment when you stop chasing and simply allow yourself to be.

I've come to realise that life won't always feel light and that's okay. Because even in the ordinary, even in the pauses between joy and struggle, there's a quiet rhythm that reminds you you're still here, still whole.

Contentment isn't the absence of desire; it's the peace that stays while you wait for what's meant for you. It's that soft exhale when you stop trying to make life happen faster than it's meant to.

And maybe that's where the secret lies — not in endless smiles or perfect days, but in the gentle acceptance that even now, even here, life is enough.

That's where happiness becomes —

Beyond smiles.

9
The PERMA Of My Journey

"Sometimes, we don't study lessons — we live them first, and only later realise they had a name."

Like I mentioned in my Author's Note, Beyond Smiles was never meant to be another self-help or psychology-heavy book. It's not about theories or formulas for happiness. It's about my journey — the heartbreaks, the healing, the rediscovery, and the quiet lessons that found me in between.

But somewhere along this journey, the concepts I studied as a counsellor began to intertwine with the life I was living. The lines blurred between the professional and the personal — between theory and experience. That's when the PERMA model stopped being a framework in a textbook and started becoming a mirror to my story.

"Happiness often sneaks in through a door you didn't know you left open." – John Barrymore

So when I first learned about the PERMA model in my Diploma of Positive Psychology, I didn't read it like a student.

I read it like someone recognising an old friend.

My lecturer said, "These are the five pillars of well-being — Positive Emotion, Engagement, Relationships, Meaning, and Accomplishment."

And as she spoke, I realised:

I had lived with each one.

Not through textbooks, but through heartbreak, substance reliance, self-doubt, and healing.

When Life Became the Classroom

When I look back now, I can see how every season of my life quietly carried a piece of PERMA before I even knew what it was called.

Positive Emotion — I used to think this meant always being happy. But now I know, it's about those small, genuine moments of peace that follow chaos.

I remember the day I felt fresh waking up in the morning and had energy to brush my teeth after months of emotional exhaustion, when I thought about someone who abandoned me and it didn't hurt anymore. I smiled — not because everything was perfect, but because I finally felt alive again. That, to me, was a positive emotion: peace after survival.

Engagement — that was what I lost when I was drowning in distraction.

After the heartbreak, I tried to fill every void — through psychics, alcohol, late-night scrolling, and chasing instant gratification. I was always running — from my pain, from my thoughts, from myself.

But when I started rebuilding, step by step, something shifted.

I began journaling again. I took long walks. I listened to my clients' stories, and I called my friends.

That's when I understood what engagement truly meant — being so present in what you're doing that healing happens without you even noticing.

Relationships — this pillar hit home.

Losing Ahaana Mama was a heartbreak that changed me forever.

She wasn't just a person in my life; she was my foundation, my peace, my mirror. Losing her wasn't just grief — it was an earthquake that shook everything I believed about love, trust, and belonging.

But that pain also taught me that love doesn't always have to stay to be real.

Some connections come to build you, and when they leave, their lessons remain etched in your soul.

Meaning — this one found me when I least expected it.

In my darkest moments, I kept asking, "Why?"

Why did I lose people? Why did I feel so lost? Why did nothing feel enough?

And the answer came slowly, because I needed to grow through it all. Because if I hadn't fallen apart, I wouldn't have learned to hold others together.

Meaning wasn't something I found; it was something that unfolded — every time I sat with someone's pain and realised I knew exactly how it felt.

Accomplishment — for the longest time, I confused this with success.

Diplomas, certificates, and milestones felt like progress, but they were only pieces of paper.

The first time a client told me, "I finally slept peacefully last night," I realised — that was the real reward.

Helping others find light in their darkness was my accomplishment.

That's when I saw it clearly — I hadn't just learned PERMA.

I had become it. Life taught me PERMA long before psychology did — it just called it survival, healing, and grace.

> *"Perhaps happiness was never meant to be pursued — only realised."*

10

Beyond Smiles

"We were never meant to smile through every storm. We were meant to live through them — and still find moments that make us smile anyway."

The Truth Behind the Smile

If you've come this far, you already know; this book didn't start from a place of perfection or constant joy. It began with a smile that didn't quite reach my eyes.

It was a smile that was desperately trying to hold itself together when everything inside felt like it was falling apart—a defense mechanism against the world and sometimes, against myself.

But now, as I sit here writing these final pages, that smile feels different.

It's no longer forced or fragile. It's gentle — born not from pretending everything is fine, but from knowing that even when it's not, I still am.

That's what *Beyond Smiles* truly means to me now.

It's no longer about putting on a brave face for the world.

It's about being real with myself — letting the mask fall, the tears flow, and the laughter rise again when it's ready.

There was a time I thought happiness was something I had to chase — through people, achievements, or milestones. I believed it was something I had to earn, to prove, to deserve. But life taught me something much softer: that happiness isn't about having everything together; it's about being together with yourself, even when everything feels uncertain.

And if you've reached this page, I want you to know something:

You don't have to chase happiness.
You just have to come home to yourself.

What I Learned About Happiness

Through this journey — through loss, love, reflection, and rediscovery — I learned that happiness is not a constant state.

It ebbs and flows, just like the ocean.

Some days, it rushes in waves of laughter and warmth.

Other days, it's quiet — a gentle tide that just reminds you to breathe.

And that's okay.

Because real happiness doesn't mean being happy all the time.

It means allowing yourself to feel all the time — joy, grief, fear, peace — and still choosing to find light within it.

From heartbreak, I learned that love doesn't end when someone leaves; it transforms into lessons, strength, and gratitude.

From comparison, I learned that peace begins the moment you stop measuring your worth by someone else's story.

From purpose, I learned that meaning can grow from even the most broken soil.

And from every quiet night of doubt, I learned that healing doesn't make you who you were — it makes you who you were always meant to be.

Now I see that happiness isn't the loud laughter in a crowded room — it's the quiet relief that fills your chest after a long cry.

It's the peace that whispers, "I'm okay now."

The Essence of 'Beyond Smiles'

When I chose the title *Beyond Smiles*, it came from a simple truth we all grow up believing — that a smile equals happiness. From childhood, we are taught to see a smile as proof that someone is okay, thriving, fulfilled. But as we move through life, we begin to realise something no one ever warned us about:
A smile can express joy…
and it can also be a mask to hide sadness just as easily.

We use it to reassure others.
We use it to protect ourselves.
We use it even when the heart behind it is tired or hurting.

And that realisation became the seed of this book.

Beyond Smiles is not about rejecting the smile — it's about understanding what exists behind it. It's about the kind of happiness that isn't dependent on expression, performance, or perfection. It's about discovering the quiet, grounded contentment that stays with you even on days when you don't have the energy to smile at all.

Happiness, I've learned, isn't proven by how we look. It's felt in how we live — gently, honestly, and fully.

The essence of this book is simple:
True happiness lives beyond the smile.
It lives in the moments when you're real with yourself, with or without an expression to show for it.

And when you learn to find peace there — behind the smile, beneath the mask, within yourself — that's when happiness truly becomes yours.

One Last Message to You

Before you close this book, I want to leave you with this:

You are not meant to have life figured out all at once.
You are not required to be unbreakable.
You are not falling behind.
You are simply human — beautifully, imperfectly, wonderfully human.

If there's one thing I hope you take away from these pages, it's this:
Your happiness is not fragile.
It does not depend on a perfect moment, a perfect person, or a perfect version of you.
It grows in your honesty, your courage, your softness, and your ability to sit with yourself — even on the days you feel uncertain.

You don't have to smile to prove anything.
You don't have to hide to protect others.
You don't have to rush your becoming.

You are allowed to take your time.
You are allowed to choose yourself.
You are allowed to outgrow the life that taught you to shrink your emotions.

And above all — you are allowed to build a happiness that is yours, even in silence, even in softness, even in moments when your smile is resting.

Thank you for walking this journey with me.
Thank you for letting my words meet you where you are.
And thank you — truly — for choosing to go *beyond smiles* with me.

Wherever life takes you next, I hope you carry one truth gently with you:

You deserve a happiness that feels real — not performed, not borrowed, not dependent... just yours.

And I hope you find it, not somewhere far ahead, but right here,
inside you,
in the now.

Closing Reflection

As you reach the end of these pages, I want to invite you into a gentle pause — a moment to breathe, to settle, and to simply *be* with everything this book has stirred within you.

Beyond Smiles was never meant to give you instructions for happiness.
It was meant to open a door — inward.

A door to the parts of yourself you may have rushed past.
A door to the truths you've softened for too long.
A door to the quiet corners of your heart that have been waiting for you to sit with them, listen to them, and finally honour them.

If there is one thing this journey has taught me, it's that happiness doesn't arrive all at once.
It's not a finish line you cross or a prize you win.
It's something you collect in moments — small ones, imperfect ones, often the ones no one else notices.

It's in the strength it takes to keep going.
It's in the honesty of admitting how you feel.
It's in the softness you offer yourself after years of being hard on your own heart.
It's in the quiet confidence of knowing you don't need to perform your joy to make it real.

Through writing this book, I learned that healing is not a dramatic transformation — it's a series of gentle shifts.
Tiny recalibrations.
Moments of awareness that bloom into change.

And perhaps the most beautiful truth of all:
Happiness isn't something you chase. It's something you grow.

Inside your choices,
inside your perspective,
inside your willingness to let yourself be seen — by others, and especially by yourself.

As you close this book, I hope it leaves you with more than comfort.

I hope it leaves you with clarity.
Not about the future — but about *you*.

About your strength, your worth, your resilience, your ability to build a life that feels like home — even in the quiet, even in the uncertainty, even when your smile is soft or missing.

And if you forget the lessons, return to them gently.
Not as rules, but as reminders.

Happiness lives within you.
Maybe not loudly.
Maybe not every day.
But deeply — and always.

Thank you for letting me walk beside you in these pages. May your life beyond this book be full of truth, tenderness, and a joy that doesn't need an audience to be real.

This is your journey now — beyond the smiles, into yourself.

EPILOUGE

In 2020, I was diagnosed with Depression and Generalised Anxiety Disorder (GAD).
That year didn't just change my life — it broke it open.

The unraveling didn't happen suddenly. It didn't come with warning signs or dramatic moments. It happened quietly, slowly, in tiny pieces I didn't notice until one day I woke up and no longer recognised myself. The version of me who once laughed loudly, loved openly, and cared deeply had slipped away somewhere between sleepless nights and tear-soaked mornings.

Some days, brushing my teeth felt impossible. Some nights, lifting my head from the pillow felt like a battle I didn't have the strength to fight. I reached for alcohol not to celebrate, but to escape — to numb the noise, silence the overthinking, and find even a moment of relief. And there were nights I cried in prayer, begging God to take this life away because I didn't know how to keep going inside a body that felt heavy and a mind that refused to rest.

That's the thing about depression:
It doesn't always look like sadness.
Sometimes it looks like functioning.
Sometimes it looks like silence.
Sometimes it looks like me.

Anxiety tightened its grip around everything — my chest, my breath, my thoughts. I lived every second waiting for the next spiral. Even in moments of stillness, my mind was anything but quiet.

And then…
Ahaana Mama came into my life.

I didn't know it then, but she was the turning point of everything. She arrived like a whisper from the universe — soft, steady, grounding. With her calm voice and gentle presence, the world felt less frightening. Life felt less heavy. I felt less alone.

Around her, I could breathe again. I could laugh. I could cry without shame. I could be messy, childish, silly, unapologetically myself. She became my safety, my solace, my reminder that life still had softness left in it. She didn't just help me heal; she made me feel alive again.

And then…
I lost her.

Losing Ahaana Mama wasn't just painful — it was devastating.
It wasn't the kind of heartbreak you move on from in weeks or months.
It was the kind that shatters your identity, fractures your self-worth, and leaves a wound that echoes through every part of your life.

Her absence broke me in a way nothing and no one ever had.
It was the loss that pushed me into the darkest chapters of this book.
The loss that led to the diagnosis.

The loss that collapsed my world.
The loss that shaped the woman who eventually learned to rise again.

But here is the truth I never expected to understand:

Even the deepest heartbreak can become a beginning.

Because when I look back now, I don't see a girl who failed —
I see a girl who survived.
A girl who learned to rebuild not because she felt strong, but because she had no other choice.
A girl who learned to carry pain without letting it consume what was left of her.

Ahaana Mama didn't stay forever,
but her impact did.
She reminded me of what love feels like when it's pure.
What connection feels like when it's safe.
What life feels like when it's held gently.

And because of her — even through the grief — I found my way back to myself.

Now, when I look at my story, I don't regret any part of it.

Not the pain.

Not the heartbreak.

Not the nights I collapsed into God's hands.

And not the losses that forced me to rebuild.

Every experience shaped me.

Every person changed me.

Every moment prepared me.

I survived the worst of what life had to offer.

And now I truly believe —

only good things are meant to come.

Maybe that's what discovering true happiness really is.

Not living a life without pain,

but finding meaning through it.

Not avoiding loss,

but growing from it.

Not chasing smiles,

but learning to go beyond them.

Beyond smiles, I found myself.

Acknowledgement of Inspiration

Throughout my journey, I found wisdom and comfort in the words of those who walked this path long before me.

Viktor Frankl's Man's Search for Meaning taught me the power of finding purpose even in pain.

Michael A. Singer's The Untethered Soul reminded me that peace isn't found in control, but in release.

Positive Psychology — through the teachings of Dr. Martin Seligman — helped me understand that flourishing isn't about constant happiness, but about meaning, engagement, and resilience.

These works became quiet companions through my healing — shaping not just this book, but the person I've become.

References

- Frankl, Viktor E. Man's Search for Meaning. Beacon Press, 2006.

- Singer, Michael A. The Untethered Soul: The Journey Beyond Yourself. New Harbinger Publications, 2007.

- Seligman, Martin E.P. Flourish: A Visionary New Understanding of Happiness and Well-being. Free Press, 2011. (Positive Psychology & PERMA Model)

About the Author

Michelle Mushtaq is a counsellor, CBT and NLP practitioner, and mental health advocate based in Australia.

Through her practice, The Healing Journey, Michelle has dedicated her life to helping people rediscover themselves — guiding them toward self-awareness, resilience, and inner peace.

Her approach blends psychology with compassion, bridging the science of healing with the art of being human. With training in Advanced Counselling, Positive Psychology, and Psychodynamic Psychotherapy, she believes that healing isn't about "fixing" yourself — it's about coming home to who you truly are.

Beyond her work as a therapist, Michelle is also the host of the podcast Cognitive Connection with Michelle and the founder of Michelle Mindshift Mastery on YouTube, where she explores emotional wellness, purpose, and authentic living.

Beyond Smiles: Discovering True Happiness is her first book — a deeply personal memoir and reflection of her journey through depression, loss, rediscovery, and healing. With raw honesty and gentle wisdom, she opens her heart to remind readers that happiness isn't found in perfection, but in presence — in embracing every shade of who we are, beyond smiles.

www.ingramcontent.com/pod-product-compliance
Lightning Source LLC
Chambersburg PA
CBHW062048290426
44109CB00027B/2769